howto marketing

series of business self-help books written by practitioners

the little cook book of email marketing

by Thom Poole

written by Thomas F Poole © 2012 Thom Poole

first published by Lulu in 2012

ISBN: 978-1-4716-4516-7

for Emma
for your support in my digital marketing career

contents

the little cook book of email marketing

what is *email marketing*?

> *email marketing* is using email to distribute your *marketing* messages.
>
> *Chris Garrett*

what is said of *email marketing*

the Chartered Institute of *Marketing* (CIM) says...

> *email marketing* has been a core tool in digital *marketing* for many years but it is often unable to achieve its full potential due to a lack of guidance in best practice, issues with spam and the changing way in which we use *email.*

the American *Marketing* Association (AMA) says...

> *email marketing* is one of the most cost effective and powerful forms of digital *marketing* yet is often misunderstood by marketers and even dismissed in favour of experimentation with social media. for the seasoned digital marketer, *email marketing* often forms the basis of a comprehensive, permission-based online *marketing* strategy with a high return on investment.

> **people don't want to be 'marketed to'; they want to be 'communicated with.'**
>
> *Flint McGlaughlin*

email come into existence in the 1990's as the internet was starting to become more popular. businesses quickly figured out this was a great way to reach customers. it was also less expensive than mailing out advertisements to homes. by 1995 the number of *email* advertisements sent out that year was more than the number sent out by regular mail. businesses spend a great deal of money creating *email marketing* campaigns that won't be confused with spam.

in fact, *email marketing* hit a huge road block when spam filters became so popular. many *email marketing* campaigns had to be revamped as the filters were wiping them out. businesses were losing money on the marketing campaigns and not getting any results. however savvy computer programmers and businesses soon learned that effective *email marketing* titles and headlines as well as using their real *email* address helped get the *emails* past the various spam filters.

source: Len Hutton – ocmodshop.com

roles of *email marketing*

the term *email marketing* is usually used to refer to:

- sending *email* messages with the purpose of enhancing the relationship of a merchant with its current, previous or possible customers, to encourage customer loyalty and repeat business

- sending *email* messages with the purpose of acquiring new customers or convincing current customers to purchase something immediately

- adding advertisements to *email* messages sent by other companies to their customers

source: wikipedia.org

size of the market:

researchers estimate that US companies will spend $77 billion on interactive marketing by 2016, of which almost $2.5 billion will be *email marketing*, over double that of 2011.

source: Forrester Research

email boasts an impressive reach with 90% of respondents in Germany, Italy, France and the Netherlands subscribed to newsletters. the percentage of subscribers in the UK and Spain was lower at 70%.

source: eCircle survey

scope of *email marketing*

email marketing helps to set up *marketing* goals; develop *marketing* policies; organise *marketing* functions; put *marketing* procedures and strategies in action; and check out the online programmes in the final analysis. as a result, the scope of *email marketing* addresses the following activities comprising:

- *email marketing* sets up *marketing* goals

- evaluates the online *marketing* opportunities

- making plans for the above

- providing the effectual *marketing* organisation

- preparing and supervising the stocks at optimal levels with the intention that the customer demand can meet seamlessly

- forming and maintaining the efficiency in the activities of publicity, advertising, credit control and after-sales services

- assessing and lining up *marketing* efforts

why is *email marketing* important?

"although your time and attention are finite, the demands on your time and attention are infinite.

Merlin Mann

benefits of *email marketing*

a carefully considered *email marketing* campaign is probably one of the most cost effective *marketing* activities you can implement with the ability to measure return on investment and the opportunity to collate important data.

it can help drive traffic to your website and allow you the opportunity to evaluate visitor behaviour. used well, this inform- ation will help you tailor your products or services to your target market. a successful campaign will increase customer loyalty; encourage repeat business and attract new customers – it will also help save a few trees!

the medium of *email marketing*

email is a very versatile medium. formats range from simple text to html and rich media, including images and video. content can be one-size-fits-all or highly customised for the recipient. frequency can consist of fixed, frequent intervals or sporadic intervals, with transmissions occurring only to communicate something newsworthy. sophistication (and cost) can be very low or very high.

number of accounts		
2,900,000,000	750,000,000	300,000,000
number of messages/updates per day		
188,000,000,000	60,000,000	140,000,000
average number of messages/updates per account per day		
64.8	0.08	0.47

email around the world

there are expected to be 3.8 billion *email* accounts.

75% of all *email* accounts belong to consumers, but business users send and recieve 110 messages daily on average. some statistics about *emails* are as follows:

- 14% of all *email* accounts are in the USA
- 23% of all *email* accounts are in Europe
- 47% of all *email* accounts are in Asia/Pacific
- 18% of all *emails* received is spam, but 27% is never received

the little cook book of email marketing

the ingredients of *email marketing*

> " there are no magic wands, no hidden tricks, and no secret handshakes that bring you immediate success, but with **time**, **energy**, and **determination** you can get there. "
>
> *Darren Rowse*
> *founder - problogger*

the *email marketing* mix

email marketing is a mix of **attention, engagement** and a **call to action**. because of the negativity of the image of *email* thanks to spam, it is important to get the ingredients right.

the *email marketing* mix comprises of:

- the audience
- title
- content
- call-to-action
- measurement

audience

chosing your audience for your campaign takes time and should not be rushed. in *marketing*, we talk about segmentation, targeting and positioning:

- *segmentation* of the list of customers or prospects
  this arranges the list into homogeneous segments

- *targeting* of a particular segment for a particular message, product or medium
  this ensures that the audience are most receptive to the message or product

- *positioning* of an image or identity for the product, brand or message in the minds of the target audience

target audiences are best understood through specific research resulting in a specific profile of the audience. this research should answer at least the following questions about the target audience:

- who/where are they (demographics)?

- how do they get their information?

- who are their role models?

- what are their current perceptions, knowledge, needs, wants, preferences, and behaviour in relation to the issue addressed by the campaign?

- what is preventing them adopting an alternative behaviour promoted by the campaign?

- what would motivate them to adopt the promoted behaviour?

the more diverse a target audience is (e.g. general public), the more difficult it is to answer the above questions. without the answers to these questions, it is almost impossible to create the right messages, chose the appropriate communication tools, and offer the specific incentives that will enable a campaign strategy to successfully achieve the desired change in behaviour.

lists

you can build mailing lists in two broad ways – organically, or by purchasing lists from others.

organic lists – are built using in-house methods. it is often slower, but provides better results as customers want the information.

methods of growing mailing lists organically include:

- *email* sign-up form prevalent on your website, social media sites and other online channels
- clearly outline the benefits for signing up
- ensure your subscribers of your commitment to privacy
- offer a variety of *email* frequency options (daily, weekly, monthly)
- offer a variety of *emails* (promotions, news, whitepapers, webinars)
- ensure that you'll respect subscribers' *email* preferences and frequency
- ensure that your *email* opt-in form is quick and simple, and if you want more information about them, keep it optional

the little cook book of email marketing

the biggest benefits of growing your own list organically are:

- preventing 'telemarketer syndrome'
  this is where customers get unwanted *emails* (spam) that they didn't want, sign up for, and are often poorly targeted

- build customer trust
  when someone signs up for your information, newsletter or product, you start building trust. buying a list does not imply that you are buying the trust of the customer

- reinforce your online *marketing* strategy
  organically grown lists are a reflection on the effectiveness of your overall online marketing strategy. if your activities are engaging, you will get a larger, more robust list

- prevents *email* list fatigue
  if you control the list, you know how often it is used for communications, so you can prevent any overloads of information going to each customer

source: simplycast.com

purchased lists – a quick fix that is ideal when you are launching a new product, service or brand and don't have the luxury of time.

using established lists from reputable brokers can help research the market, or reach otherwise unattainable customers. purchasing a list can also provide the opportunity to build business partnerships.

the thing to ensure when buying a list is that the broker is credible. it is not in the interests of credible brokers to overuse a list and therefore create fatigue. some lists could be the opposite and not current due to lack of usage and therefore full of dead links.

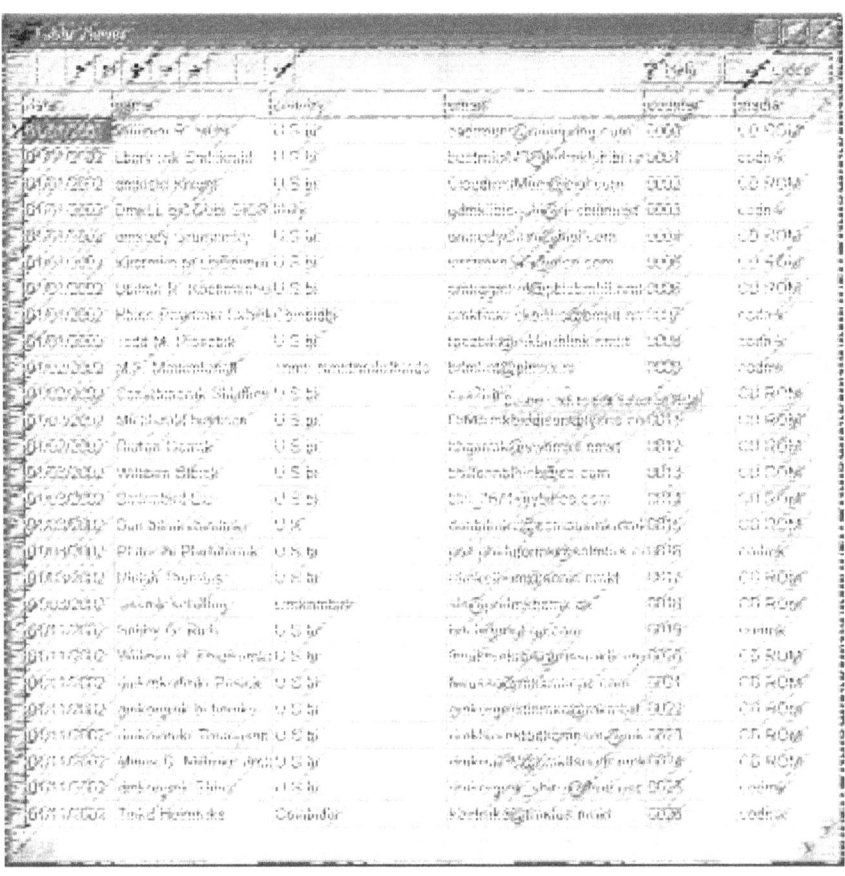

when to send *emails*

timing is everything, and if you get everything else right, but send the message out at the wrong time, you are likely to fail. this guide comes from *email marketing* company – Pure360:

 10pm to 9am

the abyss

an ineffective time to send *email* promotions

 9am to 10am

customer am

the second most popular time when customer are most receptive to offers on a whole range of subjects

 10am to noon

do not disturb

customers are focused on work and catching up on business *emails* – they are less likely to respond to promotions

 noon to 2pm

lunchtime news

customers are more likely to spend time on news and magazine alerts during lunchtime than opening marketing *emails*

2pm to 3pm

in the zone

in the immediate post-lunch period, customers remain focused on work but do respond to well targeted *emails*

3pm to 5pm

a life changing afternoon

job-related apathy can set in, meaning more *emails* relating to non-business promotions are likely to be opened

5pm to 7pm

working late

there is a dramatic rise in personal promotions being opened. this can, however be a good timeframe where recipients are most likely to open b2b promotions, if they are in the office

7pm to 10pm

last orders

consumer promotions are more likely to be well received at this time. business messages may be differed until the morning, and then lost

if promoting internationally, adjust your promotions for timezones, and for culture – e.g. middle eastern countries start their weekend on Thursdays, but work on Sundays!

how often should you send *email* promotions?

this is a difficult question to answer because it depends on a number of factors:

- what have you promised the customer?
- what preferences has the customer given, if any?
- what the nature of your business is
- how else you use/sell the list

the DMA national client *email marketing* report shows an increase in frequency of *emails*, although it does not identify the success of these campaigns.

this is all about getting the balance right between *email* overexposure and underexposure. with overexposure, the recipient receives too many *emails* from a company that they don't have time to read, or feel they are being spammed. they become 'emotionally unsubscribed'.

underexposed means that opportunities and sales are lost as the customer receives insufficient *emails*.

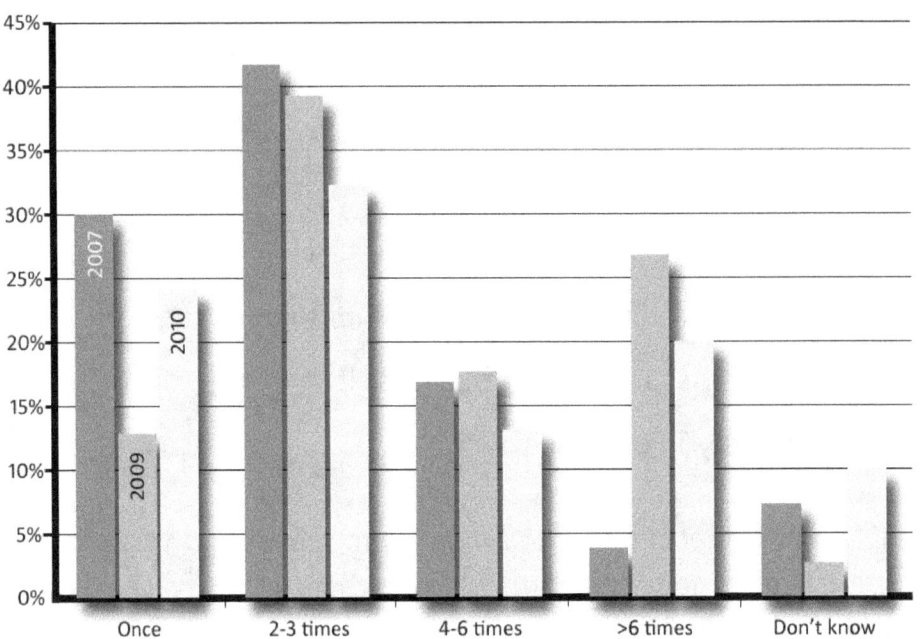

the graph shows the maximum number of times business contacted an address on their list in one month. source: UK DMA.

an econsultancy report showed that the average frequency of *email* delivery by US e-retailers was 2.5 *emails* per week, 11 *emails* per month – an average of 132 per year.

the little cook book of email marketing

measure *email* frequency success

every company will need different frequencies for their communications – possibly even within each company and strategic business unit. you will generally need to undertake additional analysis to try to identify the following:

- average frequency of *emails* received and plot the profile by frequency for diferent list members. this will demonstrate the proportion of the list who are receiving too many, or too few *emails*

- list activity – the open rate, click through and purchase rates within a campaign or time period

- recency of the response – when was the last time the recipient opened a message, clicked through or purchased. it makes sense to store this information

- break down the list activity and recency measures by different types of list members – different frequencies work for different segments

- break down the list activity by the time on the list – it is thought that the longer the time on the list, especially without purchasing anything, the less responsive the *emails* become.

source: Dave Chaffey – smartinsights 2011

digital *marketing* allows marketers to test theories via multi-variant techniques. this means that a list owner can test the best frequencies for their lists.

Chaffey recommends the following options to identify the optimum frequency:

- **reduce *email* frequencies automatically for lower responding customers**
  use the customer database to record the activity or engagement level for each customer. Amazon is a good example of this

- **change the frequency for different segments**
  one size does not fit all, and different segments will need different treatment

- **give customers a choice on frequency**
  use their profile or a communications preference centre to give customers the option to change content or frequency preferences.
  in research i carried out some years ago, customers were happy to increase the frequency of communications in exchange for additional services

the little cook book of email marketing

- **increase direct mail for customers with a lower *email* response**
  called 'right channelling' this uses a form of multi-variant testing in which a small group doesn't receive the communications at all

- **re-engagement campaigns**
  re-activiation campaigns use content or discounts to encourage *email* subscribers to become active again

email subject line

the subject line of an *email* is vital to the success of a campaign. it is possible to write long subject lines, but only the first fifty characters stand out.

to make the *email* stand out, there are some simple rules:

1. **read a newspaper**
   headlines in newspapers are designed, like subject lines in *emails*, to engage the reader and encourage them to read the articles

2. **there is no sure-fire formula**
   what works with one campaign may not work for a different one. a discount that worked once may not have the same effect again. if you can repeat successes, all well and good

3. **test, test, test**
   test continually to determine trends and styles that work. pretest campaigns if possible

4. **support the 'from' line**
   the 'from' line shows who sent the *email*. if your 'from' line contains your company name, it shouldn't be repeated in the subject line. use your brand to make your subject line stand out. make your 'from' come from a person, rather than 'sales@' or 'info@'

5. **list key information first**
   some *email* clients display more characters in the subject line, but the rule of thumb is 50 characters. look to the 'above the line' (atl) content – the information that appears in the first screen, without the need to scroll down a page

6. **open rates aren't indicative of successful subject-lines**
   your end goal is not to get high open rates, but to react to the call-to-action (cta) in the *email*. good open rates can be seen as an indication, but should not be the guiding factor

7. **personalise**
   personalised subject lines based on the recipients product or content preferences, interests, past purchases, web visits or links clicked can encourage increased engagement. care should be taken when mentioning past purchases as they could have been gifts or there may have been a problem with the purchase

8. **urgency drives action**
   set a deadline – use of urgency and deadlines can increase the open rate. it can also alienate recipients if over- or improperly used

9. **watch out for those spam filters**
   there is often a fine line between 'catchy' and 'spammy' headlines. there are numerous content checkers that will highlight possible spam content. there are numerous lists available of potential spam works and phrases

the little cook book of email marketing

10. 'free' is not evil

it is often said that you can't use the word 'free' in the subject line – this is not true, but don't make it the first word, write it in capitals or punctuate it with an exclamation mark. 'free' can be highly emotive

11. lead, but don't mislead

don't stretch the truth in the subject line or over promise – you should build trust with the communications. if your *email* content does not reflect the subject line, it is likely to be caught by the spam or junk filters

12. write and test early and often

the subject line is often the last and a hurried step in an *email* campaign – it should be the other way around. subject lines should be tested, ideally with segments of your audience

13. review subject-line performance over your last campaigns

review which *email* subject lines work – give the highest conversion rates, average sales, click-through rates. remember, a website visit or purchase (on or offline) could be as a result of cumulative *email* campaigns

14. continue the conversation

create a conversation with your readers. adapt what you say to the responses you get from your 'conversations'. if your *email* frequency allows it, continue the dialogue from previous *emails*

15. can you pass the must-open/must-read test?

people no longer open everything that appears in their inboxes – they need to be intrigued.

the must-read test – if a subscriber doesn't open the *email* they will feel that they missed out, and regret their inaction

the unbulk bulk folder test – if the *email* goes into the bulk or junk folder, does the combination of sender (from) and subject line inspire trust that leads the recipient to move it to their inboxes

source: lyris.com

content

an *email marketing* programme exists to add to the organisations financial success. this may be through sales, brand awareness, relationship building or fundraising. generating *email marketing* roi is your ultimate goal.

people want special deals, exclusive offers and time-limited promotions. but all content – even if they are offering customers something, should be relevant. how often do you want a two-for-one meal offer from a single restuarant?

if your *emails* only sell, you'll wear out your welcome in the inbox. focus on great content as much as you focus on great offers.

engaging content solves problems for recipients – every business *email* should get to the point immediately. most recipients get far more *emails* than they can process, best practice tell us that for content over 200 words long, the reader should be transferred back to the website.

producing engaging content is about interacting with subscribers and customers in a way that makes them feel wanted and connected with your brand.

the little cook book of email marketing

tips to create more engaging *email marketing* campaigns:

- **personalise on every possible level**

  creating personal content that is tailored to suit your recipient's interests and needs. this means that you must understand your customers and how to segment them.

  successful *email marketing* is not just about the right content, it's about sharing the right content with the right audience

- **test your content**

  testing the content that resonates is important to your recipients, just as you do with the subject line. it is often the subject line and first line of the *email* that counts. test, test, test

the little cook book of email marketing

- **product content that is clear**

    this may seem obvious, but many *email* campaigns suffer from weak content, lacking direction or calls to action, are sloppy or vague.

    think about what your readers want to know, do or see. bombarding them with mixed, multiple or irrelevant messages will only lead to resentment and confusion.

- **get social**

    creating *email marketing* campaigns that are engaging enough to make them social network-friendly. a recent study on CEO online claimed that a social media option on an *email* campaign generates a 30% higher click through rate than those without.

    source: digitalfire.co.za

call-to-action

a call-to-action is the request or direction to do something within an advertisement or *marketing* campaign. this is often the 'next step' towards the puchase of a product or service.

in the interactive world of digital media, a call to action can be part of a hyperlink to access the website or subscription form – but, do not just have a redundant 'click here' in your text; make the link more descriptive, such as 'click here for our latest catalogue'.

a call-to-action provides:

- focus to your message, campaign or site

- a way to measure your site, message or campaign's success

- gives direction for your readers

10 techniques to create an effective call-to-action are:

1. **lay the groundwork**

   before a user is willing to complete a call-to-action they have to recognise the need. you may also need to communicate the benefits of responding.

2. **offer a little extra**

   sometimes you may have to sweeten the deal to encourage users to complete a call-to-action. these incentives could be discounts, competition entry or a free gift.

3. **have a small number of distinct actions**

   it is important to be focused in your call-to-action. too many and the readers become overwhelmed. there is no right number – a single one would be best, but two or three may also be acceptable.

4. **use active urgent language**

   a call-to-action should clearly tell readers what you want them to do. using words such as call; buy; register; subscribe or donate are good.

   creating a sense of urgency and the need to act can be even more powerful. words such as 'offer expires March 31st', 'for a short time only'.

5. **get the position right**

   position your call-to-action in the right place on the page. as westerners read from the top left, the best place is a high central location. there is nothing wrong with repeating the offer again at the bottom of the message.

the little cook book of email marketing

6. **use white space**

   the position is important (see previously), but if it is swamped there, the message can be lost. making sure there is space around the call-to-action will draw more attention to it.

7. **use an alternative colour**

   colour is an effective way to emphasise elements, esepecially if the message has a limited palette. never rely solely on colour, especially when the contrast is low.

8. **make it big**

   along with position, space and colour – a call-to-action that appears in a larger pitch than surrounding text will stand out better.

9. **have a call-to-action on every page**

   match the call-to-action on any landing pages you may send the readers to. the worst thing you can do is to be inconsistent in your message. also ensure that the reader doesn't reach a deadend without responding to your call.

10. **carry the call through**

    if you've done all the work to get customers to act, you must be able to follow up on your promise.

    if you collect data from customers, ensure that you don't collect unnecessary information at an early stage – you've got them to react, now close that deal before moving on to the next.

    source: Paul Boag – boagworld.com

it is much easier to double your business by doubling your
conversion rate than doubling your traffic.

Jeff Eisenberg

the little cook book of email marketing

write to engage

when you write the copy for your email marketing campaign, remember who you are writing to – the reader, customer, prospect.

to write compelling copy, keep in mind the way you can keep the attention of your reader.

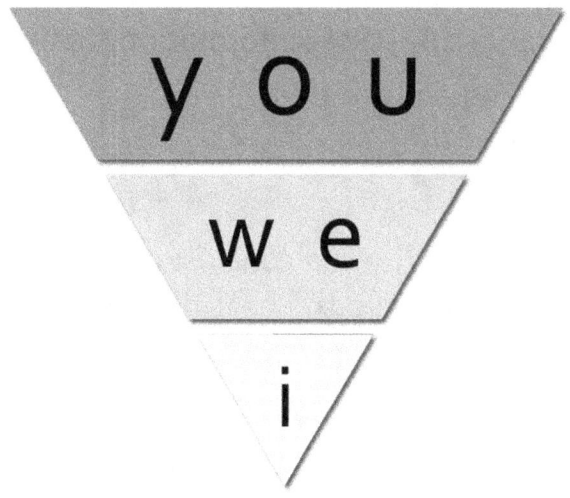

source: Alfred Tack, 1972

the image above is the **'you'** appeal logo. to influence minds, always write content in terms of the recipient's interest (**you**) or your joint interests (**we**). only rarely should you bring in your own interests (**i**) – your customer is rarely interested.

when you write: **your** business; **your** shop; **your** profits; **your** problems – you are influencing someone's mind to continue reading.

writing compelling content

- create a sense of urgency (see earlier)
- highlight the benefits of your product/service
- specify a strong call-to-action
- follow the 80-20 rule – 80% information, 20% promotion
- check all spelling and grammar
- test, test, test

just as journalists often write the conclusion first, *email* copywriters should do similar – don't save the best till last, people may not get that far!

setting the main content and call-to-action 'above the fold' (a term borrowed from the print industry) will get you more attention. research has shown that 80% of reader's time is spent in this area.

when testing your *email* messages, consider what is shown in teh preview pane, and nowadays, what can be seen on smartphone *email* clients. if your key message isn't visible, you run the risk of being ignored. positioning the most exciting/appealing/interesting content 'above the fold' will help achieve higher open rates.

getting started with your content

great content isn't always easy to create – here are some tricks to help you.

1. become a journalist

   newspapers are easy to scan. paragraphs are no more than one or two sentences long. use white space to make things easier to scan.

2. use proper grammar and punctuation

   although *emails* can be seen as less formal, grammar and punctuation still matters. well-written *emails* make a strong first and lasting impression.

3. go easy on the acronyms

   many hi-tech companies are notorious for their overuse of acronyms. if you must use industry acronyms, explain them at least once, and in *marketing* communications, refrain from using popular, consumer code.

4. don't shout

    use of all upper–case words is seen as shouting in digital circles. it is fine to emphasise a single word (if using plain text *emails*), but should not be used in html formats. all capitals also makes the text difficult to read – dyslexics have a problem distinguishing between capitalised words.

5. behave

    be mindful of your manners in the content and the urgency of your communications.

6. be circumspect

    legally, data protection legislation does not apply to b2b communications, but remember every business person is also a consumer and will be used to the privacy they enjoy there. do not abuse anyone's privacy, anywhere in the world.

7. choose your subject

    the subject line is the start of your communication – don't forget it.

8. lighten up

    long *emails*, or large attachments and pictures will detract from your message. the longer an *email* takes to load, the less likely people are to read it, and it blocks the *email* client from something the recipient may consider more important!

9. repeat yourself

    tell readers what you've told them – repeat the call-to-action.

readability of your *email* campaign

readability is the ease in which text can be read and understood.
various factors to measure readability have been used, such as
"speed of perception," "perceptibility at a distance," "perceptibility
in peripheral vision," "visibility," "the reflex-blink technique," "rate
of work" (e.g., speed of reading), "eye movements," and "fatigue in
reading."

source: wikipedia.org

to make the *email* campaign more readable, there are three quick fixes:

1. *alignment* - there is a tendency to align all text centrally. this just makes it difficult to read.

   fix: align all text to the left – don't get fancy.

2. *scannability* - if everything is in the same font, it makes it difficult to stand out. i am not advocating using different fonts, but using emphasis like bold or italic helps key information stand out.

   fix: empahsise where you want the reader's eyes to stop. but do not use underlining to emphasise on an *email* – it is not a link!

3. *line length* - when lines of text go all the way across the page, it is less inviting to read and can cause eye fatigue. this is more common with back-lit screens than on paper.

   fix: keep paragraphs and therefore lines short – perhaps 12 to 14 words.

email campaign metrics

undertaking your campaigns is only half the job. in modern business everything is tracked, and every expenditure must be evaluated. *email marketing* campaigns are [or should be] no different. so what can be measured, and what should be measured?

these are the common *email marketing* metrics:

- **messages sent**: the number of outbound *emails* sent as part of the mailing

- **messages delivered**: not all messages sent reach an inbox. such messages are deemed to have bounced
  hard bounce: is a permanently undeliverable *email*, for example for a closed or mistyped address. remove these addresses from your database
  soft bounce: is a temporarily undeliverable *email*, for example to an inbox that is full, or a server that is unavailable

the little cook book of email marketing

- **unsubscribes**: these are people who decide that they no longer wish to be on your database, and therefore no longer wish to recieve any communications from you. this is also known as opting out

- **open rate**: this is the number of *emails* that were opened. it is often tracked using a 1x1 pixel image, unique to the message, but as a result, this can also be a distorted metric

- **click through rate**: if you have a hyperlink in your *email* message (you should have some, but this is for the main message or call-to-action), this metric will track how many people clicked on it

- **referral rate**: if the *email* was forwarded to a friend or colleague, this can also be tracked, showing how popular a message is

the little cook book of email marketing

improving your open rate

create more compelling from and subject lines

commonsense i know. look at the previous chapter. a good rules of thumb is to ask a question, keeping subject lines under six words and using lowercase in all but the first word and proper nouns also helps

test your subject lines

by undertaking some multi-variant testing, you can select groups of customers with particular subject lines and content. why not test it at tdifferent times of day or days of the week too?

improve your click through rates

make your content and descriptions compelling – you've got them to open the *email* – now will they read it. give them something they want to read, see and click on.

the subject line should prepare the reader for the content. you don't want to disappoint the reader immediately?

change your message format, for example with newsletter layouts. there is a good case for maintaining design norms, or disrupting the norms and surprising the reader (obviously, in a good way)

highlight what you want your readers to read and click on. this can be done with emphasising different text, using different colours or using an understanding of hot-spots in design positioning.

improve your response rate

providing a compelling reason for the recipient to act. the way you frame your story and your call to action will have a huge impact on the response rate.

optimise the landing page for your call-to-action can help improve your response rate. it is unlikely that the *email* will have a resultant response without leading the reader to do something else – this is normally on a website, so how compelling is the landing page – the images, navigation and links on the page.

email marketing tools

there are numerous companies that will offer an *email marketing* service – providing, in some cases, design/creation services, delivery and tracking/reporting. some services allow an element of self-service on their tools. some of these tools offer *email* templates.

there are a mix of desktop, server-based and service provider software. i am not going to recommend one system over the other – i have used many from expensive, professional systems to free, open-source solutions. they are tools that you use to resolve a particular problem, and some are better at, for example, sales *emails*, or e-newsletters.

other tools to consider (and often included in the more expensive solutions) include tracking and 'bounce management' tools, spam word filters and black list address checkers.

the little cook book of email marketing

email marketing recipes

> " the urgent can drown out the important "
>
> *Marissa Mayer*

there are various forms of *email* communications 'recipes', depending on the type of communications you wish to engage in. these are:

- invitation *emails*
- sales pitch *emails*
- automated reply *emails*
- product launch *emails*
- *email* newletters
- announcement *emails*
- international *email* campaigns

invitation emails

an *email* can invite the reader to an event – on- or offline. an invitation to an event such as a presentation or webinar will often provide a click through to a form to sign up to the event.

it could be that the *email* has a form within it, but this relies on the customer being able to send the information back intact, which can sometimes be problematic. it is probably better to send the reader to a customised landing page and form where you can control the experience.

many event organisers or facilitators offer their own registration forms, but these may not be the most suitable solution. this is, however, out of the scope of this book. decide for yourself how much control you want for the campaign you are running.

sales pitch emails

an *email marketing* campaign can make a good cold calling vehicle and to follow up interests. there are three types of sales *emails*:

- to send direct promotional materials to customers who have already expressed an interest in the brand or product. this could be signing up to a newsletter, or sending product specifications

- encouraging customer loyalty by interacting directly with them, strengthening the relationship with each individual customer

- advertising in the *emails* and e-newsletters of others

because the *email* campaign is directed at people who have already expressed an interest (by opting in) you can regard them as 'warm leads'. if you structure your *emails* properly and effectively, these customers will need little persuasion to take the next step. so a good call-to-action, 'tempters' such as free offers or discounts solely for *email* recipients will be more likely to generate a positive response.

automated reply emails

you've probably seen out-of-office *emails*, but you can set these automated replies for any type of *email* response. if someone signs up to a newsletter, you can send an automatic *email* thanking them for signing up and pointing them in the direction of addition information.

because these messages are sent almost immediately, the best bet is to keep them short. they are unlikely to be highly customised, and the important thing is to make sure it is sent straight away.

product launch emails

using an *email marketing* campaign to announce the launch of a new product can help create a buzz amongst advocates of your brand. one company that excels at product launch *emails* is Apple – using images and very little text. all the taking is done by the website.

email *newsletters*

an *email* newsletter is a great way to communicate with your customers regularly, providing ongoing news and interest in what you are doing. one common fault with newsletters is that people try to cram it full of information. less is definitely more when it comes to newsletters. keep the layout clean, colourful and use links back to your website to provide the depth of information and interaction.

announcement emails

in addition to announcing new products, *emails* can be used to announce almost anything in the company and marketplace. announce new appointments, new contracts, etc., to customers who are already warm to the brand.

international email *campaigns*

when you plan to roll out an international *email* campaign, you should think about the following:

- what are the main countries and languages you want to focus on?
- how much localisation is allowed/expected?
- is it possible to manage the programme centrally?
- what can you manage from a central level?
- what political issues do you expect that could arise and how are you going to deal with these?

the little cook book of email marketing

the pitfalls

one of the biggest problems with *email marketing* is that a minority abuse the medium. being cheap, it costs almost nothing to set-up and send messages. spam as it is called is the blight of modern digital communications, now extending to other forms of unsolicited communications.

data privacy rules do exist in most markets, but much of the spam is sent from un- or poorly regulated countries. poor quality *marketing* adds to the problem.

so what is spam? spam is any unsolicited message sent to *email* accounts. unsolicited can mean that the reipient never requested any information or contact; doesn't have any relationship (and often doesn't want it) with the sender; or there is no intent for the sender to anything other than verify the *email* address for their own (often criminal) ends.

elements that create spam in business (this excludes the obvious criminal communications):

- bad lists
  using *emailing* lists of people who have not opted in for information. this is even more important for purchased lists

- poor content
  using terms that have no appeal to the recipient, or that is deemed to be spam by the algorithms used by the spam filters

- too frequent, or inconsistent frequency
  messages that arrive too frequently, or at infrequent haphazardness are usually a nuisance. if the recipient isn't expecting the message, or is overwhelmed by them, it is likely to be spam

- ignored unsubscribes
  to remove oneself from a list, you shoud be able to unsubscribe. given modern database technology, this should be immediate (no excuse for it not to be), but a company that ignores unsubscribes will be cited as a spammer

- irrelevant content/message
  messages that have no relevance to the recipient are spam. the recipient may have originally given the *email* address for relevant information, but a change in their circumstances, or a change in the messages may deem them unwanted – this is not spam, per se, but if accompanied by ignoring unsubscribes will be spam (see above)

marketing communications is all about engaging with your customers – getting and maintaining their attention. you will fail to do this if:

- you are consistently off topic (or what the recipient thinks is off topic)

- you ignore your promises of topics, frequency or tonality

- abuse of privacy – many people seem to use separate *emails* for particular sign-ups, or change something in their details (spelling of their name, etc) to help them track who is selling or stealing their details (more of that later)

are you overworking your lists? sending large numbers of messages, some on topic, some off (trying to encourage cross-sell and up-sell), will lead to resentment from the recipients, and often leads to a large number of unsubscribes.

poor content quality can also alienate your recipients. a lack of a call-to-action, poor targeting, poorly written content, or too much content (i have seen sales *emails* that would print out onto ten pages – who would want to read all that?).

privacy laws

privacy laws differ around the world, but most of this is commonsense. much of the legislation is directed at the b2c market, business details are often excluded. unfortunately, this is a short-sighted business practice – all business people are als consumers!

a country that sends, and is the source of much of the world's spam has anti-spam legislation in place – the USA. Europe has some of the strictest rules that are also appiled in law. the main difference between Europe and the US are:

- types of messages

  US: can-spam act covers all commercial *email* messages whos primary purpose is the advertisement or promotion of a commercial product or service.

  EU: the directive covers all direct *email marketing* messages, including charitable and political.

- permission/opt-in requirements

  US: not required – can-spam allows direct *email marketing* messages to be sent to anyone, without permission until they explictly opt-out.

  EU: direct *email marketing* messages can only be sent to subscribers who have given their prior consent (opt-in). for b2c, this is required for all 'natural persons'. except – during a business transaction, whether it has been completed or not.

- unsubscribe/opt-out requirement

    US: every message must include opt-out instructions. the sender must honour the opt-out request within 10-days (a joke for modern database management systems!). the recipient cannot be required to pay a fee to unsubscribe.

    EU: every message must include opt-out instructions. promotional *email marketing* messages must include a valid address. for existing business relationships, an explicit opt-out must be recieved to stop the messages.

- sender identity

    US: can-spam bans false or misleading header information, including relays.

    EU: disguised or concealed idetities of senders is prohibited.

- subject line/labelling

    US: deceptive subject lines are prohibited. the subject line cannot mislead the recipient about the contents of the message. if the message is an advertisement or solicitation, this must be disclosed.

the little cook book of email marketing

- contact information/postal address

  US: a physical postal address is required, including PO or private mailbox address.

  EU: companies registered in the EU must state their company details on every electronic business communication. this must include the full name of the company and its legal form; place of registration; registration number; address of the registered office and the VAT number (if applicable). a valid reply address must also be provided every time.

- leglisation

  US: can-spam act.

  EU: opt-in directive and the data privacy directive

legal checklist

- do you have prior explicit and verifiable permission (opt-in) from the reicipient?

- does the message have:
  - o a clear and accurate sender identity?
  - o an accurate subject line?
  - o clear and easy opt-out instructions?
  - o a physical postal address and company details?
  - o a valid return address?

- have you tested that the subscription/unsubscription links work?

- have you checked the test messages carefully before posting?

- can you process the replies and any subcribers requests promptly?

source: lsoft.com

the little cook book of email marketing

the little cook book of email marketing

conclusion

"people share, read and generally engage more with any type of content when it's surfaced through friends and people they *know* and *trust*

Malorie Lucich
Facebook spokesperson

email best practice checklist

- obtain prior permission via a double opt-in subscription. send an automated and well-worded welcome message with key instructions and expectations

- test deliverability
    - use *email* authentication: check that the sender policy framework (spf), sender identity, domainkeys and dns records all correctly verify the sender
    - use a spam checker – scan the *email* message to make sure that it isn't identified as spam

- test readability
    - check the html message design and readability. it must still work if the images are blocked (if all your information is in the images, this will fail)
    - use alternative (alt) text for html messages
    - keep the subject line short and clear. 25 characters display on most *email* clients.

- provide wanted, expected, relevant and interesting messages to each recipient

- provide clear instructions on how subscribers can automatically unsubscribe (opt-out). you may want to send an automated farewell message to thank them, and to confirm the successful opting out

source: lsoft.com

the little cook book of email marketing

instead of one-way interruption, web marketing is about delivering useful content at just the precise moment that the buyer needs it.

source: David Meerman Scott

the little cook book of email marketing

about the author

Thom Poole is a professional chartered marketer who has spent his career in developing customer-centric products and services.

during the course of writing his dissertation for his *marketing* masters, Thom identified trust as being a key factor in business success, forming the basis of his first book '*Play It By Trust*'.

with a long relationship with digital *marketing*, Thom has worked for some of the most innovative global companies, as an employee and consultant.

a professor of *marketing* at Grenoble, Thom has also created the first MSc in digital *marketing*, being delivered by a London business school.

this book was written to provide a quick guide to helping individuals and businesses understand the elements, impact and benefits of *email marketing*. understanding and quantifying *email marketing* is an ongoing task, and this book is only one step on the journey.

for more information, please visit Thom's websites:

www.jack-marketing.com

www.about-marketing.co.uk

other titles in the howto marketing series:

the little cook book of email marketing